# SUNDIATA
## THE SELF - DETERMINED KING

Written by Doreen N. Myrie Ed.D

# Dedication

For my beloved parents, who loved me beyond words.

-D.N.M

Long, long ago, in a faraway land called Mali, there was a little boy named Sundiata. He was born into a royal family, which meant his father was the king! But even though Sundiata was a prince, he faced many challenges.

Unlike other children, Sundiata could not walk or run. His legs were weak, and he often needed help moving around. Some people whispered and wondered if he could ever be a strong leader, but Sundiata's mother, Queen Sogolon, always believed in him.

"Sundiata, my son," she would say, "you have a strong heart and a brave spirit. One day, you will be a great king." These words made Sundiata feel strong inside, even if his legs were not.

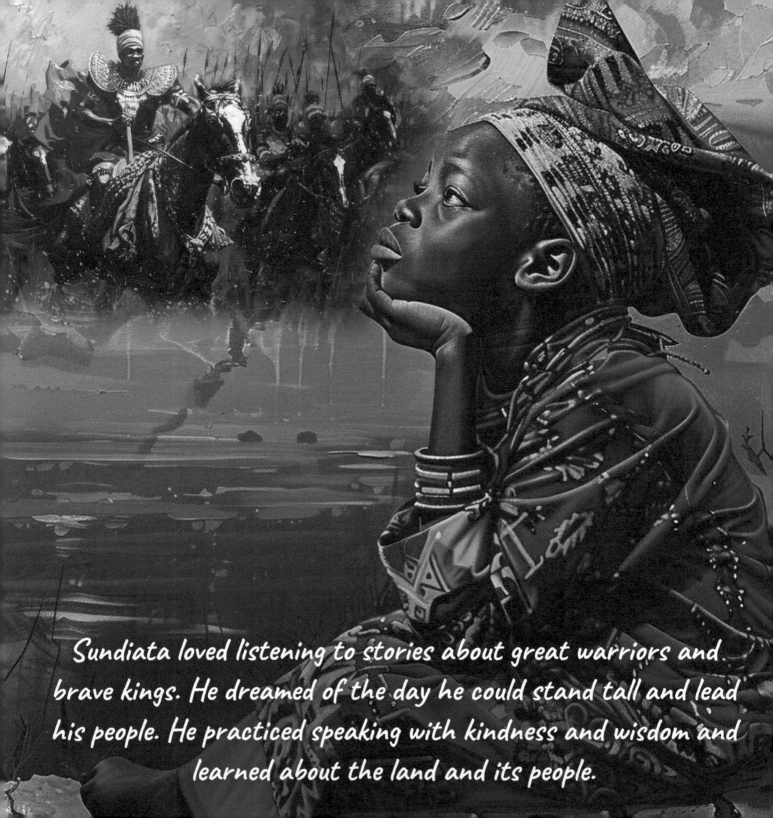

Sundiata loved listening to stories about great warriors and brave kings. He dreamed of the day he could stand tall and lead his people. He practiced speaking with kindness and wisdom and learned about the land and its people.

One sunny day, while Sundiata was sitting under a baobab tree, he saw other children playing. He wished he could join them. With determination shining in his eyes, he decided to try standing up. Slowly and carefully, he pushed himself up from the ground.

It was hard, and he stumbled many times. But Sundiata did not give up. He practiced every day. Each time he fell, he would get back up, stronger and more determined than before.

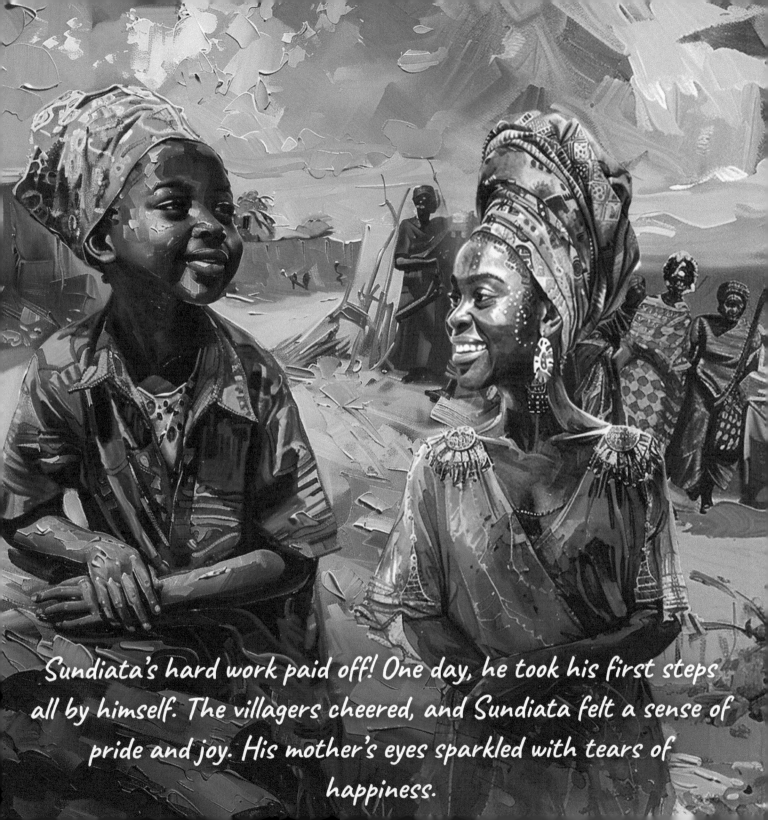

Sundiata's hard work paid off! One day, he took his first steps all by himself. The villagers cheered, and Sundiata felt a sense of pride and joy. His mother's eyes sparkled with tears of happiness.

News of Sundiata's determination spread throughout the land. People began to see him not just as a boy with weak legs but as a future king with a strong heart. They knew he would lead them with courage and wisdom.

As Sundiata grew older, his strength grew, too. He learned to ride a horse and became skilled with a bow and arrow. Despite his early challenges, he showed everyone that he could be a great warrior.

One day, a great danger threatened Mali. An enemy named Soumaoro wanted to take over the kingdom. The people were scared and needed a leader to save them.

Sundiata knew this was his moment. He gathered an army and led them bravely into battle. With his clever plans and fierce determination, he defeated Soumaoro and saved the kingdom.

The people of Mali celebrated Sundiata as their hero. They crowned him king, and he ruled with kindness and fairness. Sundiata always remembered the challenges he faced and always helped others who struggled, too.

King Sundiata's story traveled far and wide. He became known as Sundiata the Self-Determined King. Children all over the world heard his story and felt inspired by his courage and perseverance.

And so, Sundiata's legacy lived on, teaching everyone that no matter the challenges, with self-determination, we can achieve great things.

Remember, just like Sundiata, you have a strong heart and a brave spirit. Believe in yourself, and you, too can overcome any challenge!

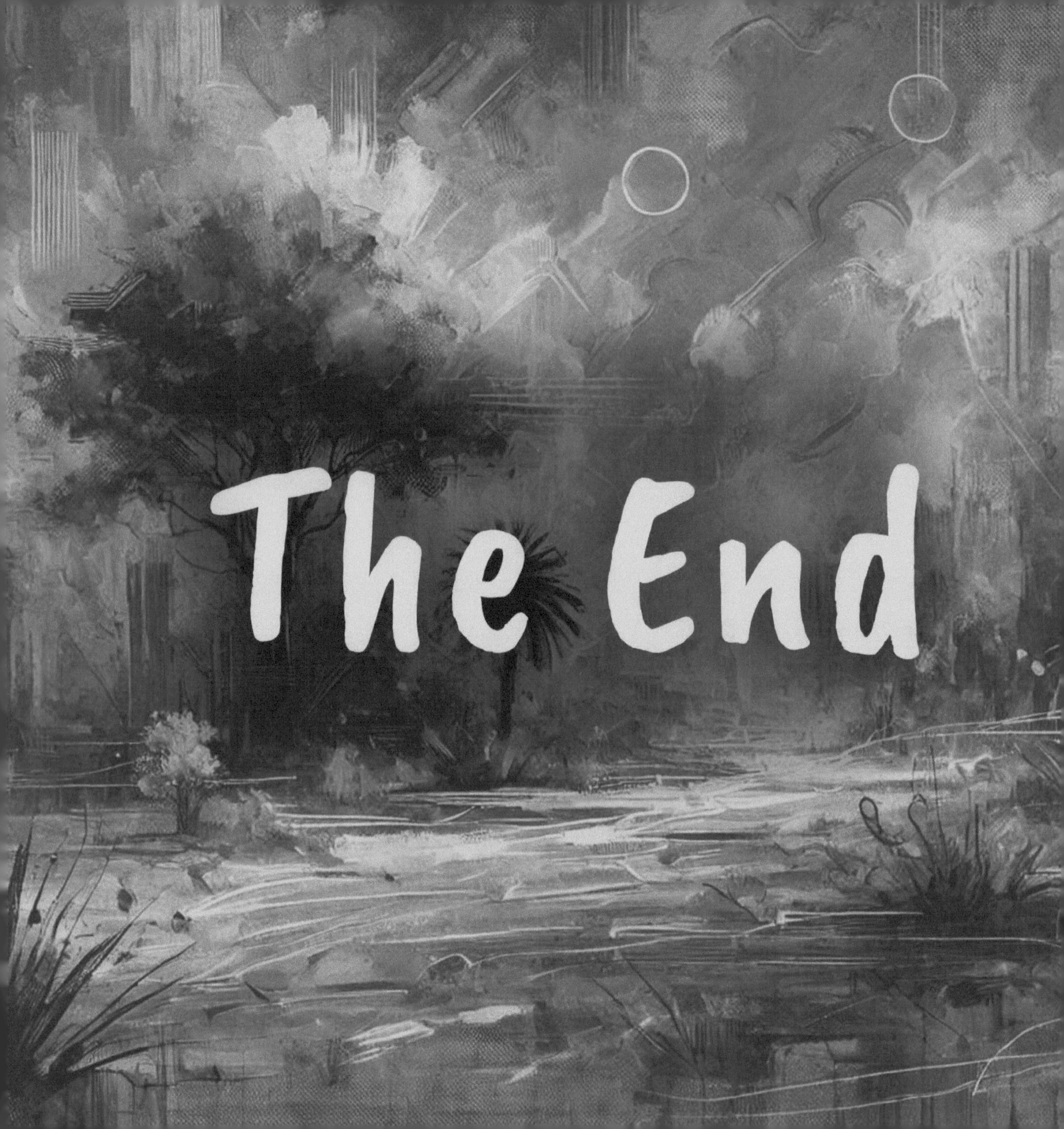
The End

# Author's Note

Dear Reader,

Sundiata Keita was a real person who lived long ago in Africa. He faced many challenges but never gave up. His story teaches us about the power of self-determination. No matter our difficulties, we can achieve great things by believing in ourselves and never giving up.

Remember, you are strong, you are brave, and you can do amazing things!

With love,
Doreen N. Myrie

# About the Author

"Dr. Doreen N. Myrie, a nature lover, is a seasoned educator and researcher with decades of experience in K-12 and teacher education. She has a passion for history and storytelling, coupled with a deep commitment to sharing cultural tales with young readers. "Sundiata the Self-Determined King" is her first children's book, inspired by the rich heritage and history of African folklore. Dr. Myrie's work often focuses on themes of resilience, self-determination, and the celebration of all abilities and cultural diversity. Through her storytelling, she aims to inspire children to embrace their heritage and believe in their potential. Dr. Myrie deeply believes in the power of stories to educate and uplift. She resides in Mississippi, USA, where she continues to teach, write, and inspire future generations.

# SUNDIATA

## THE SELF-DETERMINED KING

"Sundiata the Self-Determined King" follows the young prince Sundiata, who, despite being unable to walk or run like other children, dreams of leading his people. With the unwavering belief and support of his mother, Queen Sogolon, Sundiata embarks on a journey of self-discovery and perseverance. His determination to overcome his physical limitations ultimately leads him to become a great warrior and the savior of his kingdom from an evil sorcerer, Soumaoro. Through his trials, Sundiata becomes a symbol of strength and resilience, inspiring children to believe in themselves and their abilities. The book stands out for its unique story idea and cultural authenticity. It offers a high-interest plot line that captivates young readers while teaching them valuable lessons about courage and determination. The character of Sundiata serves as an inspiring role model for children, with and without disabilities, showing them that they can overcome any obstacle with determination and a strong spirit.

Printed in the USA
CPSIA information can be obtained
at www.ICGtesting.com
LVHW072001150924
790968LV00002B/92

* 9 7 8 9 6 9 4 9 9 2 7 7 8 *